# CRITICAL THINKING ACTIVITIES TO IMPROVE WRITING SKILLS

## Where-Abouts A1

—Books in this series—
Descriptive Mysteries
Where-Abouts
Arguments
Whatcha-Macallits

Karen Albertus • Bonnie Baker
• Michael Baker • Carole Bannes • Elizabeth Korver

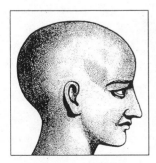

© 1989
**CRITICAL THINKING BOOKS & SOFTWARE**
www.criticalthinking.com
P.O. Box 448 • Pacific Grove • CA 93950-0448
Phone 800-458-4849 • FAX 831-393-3277
ISBN 0-89455-386-0
Printed in the United States of America

# Contents

© 1989 MIDWEST PUBLICATIONS • P.O. Box 448, Pacific Grove, CA 93950

# Teacher Suggestions

These materials offer teachers the opportunity to supplement their writing programs with easy-to-use, entertaining critical thinking activities that emphasize real-life communication skills. They are applicable to grades 4–8, and the nongraded format also allows them to be used as a remediation tool for older students.

### RATIONALE: SKILL DEVELOPMENT

Writing and following directions are difficult and complex tasks. They involve students in organizing various types of information and in using visual imagery and visual discrimination. Students must also become familiar with concepts and terminology related to orienteering. They are called upon to use precise descriptive vocabulary and to compare and contrast similar objects. All of these skills are necessary in their reading and writing if they are to communicate clearly with one another.

### ACTIVITY STRUCTURE

Each activity is constructed around a map and two different sets of Writer's Instructions, each with a more detailed small map. Students, working together in pairs, write directions for other students to follow. Directions are then exchanged and students try to find the hidden goal as instructed by their peers. Successful strategies and problem areas are discussed when the activity is finished. (See the Lesson Plan on pages 1–3 for more details.)

Levels of difficulty and complexity spiral up throughout the book. Several activities at the same level provide students with adequate practice before proceeding to more challenging maps.

Since these are supplemental materials, it is recommended that the class do no more than one map activity per day.

### STUDENT'S ROLE

Students will work in groups of four and in pairs within their groups.

After carefully examining the maps and the special Writer's Information, the pairs of students are asked to write accurate and specific directions for other students to read and follow. To do this, writers need to discriminate large and small differences; classify, compare, and contrast objects; place objects directionally and in reference to other objects; orientate themselves; and devise a usable route that will take them sequentially from a starting point to a goal. This route then has to be translated into understandable written language for others to read and follow on the map.

When both pairs in a group have completed their writing, they exchange papers. Each pair now reads the other's directions and tries to follow the described route on the map. To do this, students must read the directions and plot their route very carefully while at the same time examining the map in fine detail.

Students discover and share information, successful strategies, and problem areas with their partners, group, and, finally, with the entire class.

### TEACHER'S ROLE

One activity is provided for teacher modeling of the desired thinking processes. It includes suggested questioning strategies that can be used with students' involvement as the teacher works through a problem.

The teacher should encourage students to do some covert thinking before responding to questions and to spend time carefully examining all information they receive or provide to others. Accuracy is very important.

While monitoring independent group work, the teacher is provided feedback that indicates which students need extra help in understanding a particular concept, in developing sufficient vocabulary, or in writing and following directions. If students seem to be experiencing difficulties, a question that starts them thinking in a different direction will often allow them to proceed to a solution.

### EVALUATION

After students have completed an activity, problems and differences arising from incorrect or inaccurate answers will supply lively discussion. The feedback the teacher receives from monitoring this interplay will provide information on individual student's progress. After each activity, the teacher may wish to consider regrouping with the intention of better balancing abilities, skills, and personalities.

These materials afford students ample opportunity for self-evaluation and peer tutoring as thinking processes are verbalized in oral and written form and ideas are exchanged, then applied to the task of writing and following directions. Students are easily able to judge their own successes and difficulties from their results.

# Suggested Teaching Strategy

## PURPOSE:

√ to improve critical thinking skills by learning to write, read, and follow accurate and specific written directions

√ to improve the ability to differentiate between similar objects and describe them in detail

√ to improve the ability to evaluate effectively all steps in the process

## OBJECTIVE:

The student will write clear, precise directions for going from a starting point to a goal using landmarks, obstacles, and correct directionality points as indicators for orienteering on a map. The student will also read and follow written directions using indicators to locate a goal on a map.

## PROCEDURE:

The teacher should distribute copies of pages 4 and 5 to students and, using a chalkboard and an overhead projector, proceed to model desired thinking processes for the students. The following activity models types of questions that might be asked and methods of description that might be used. Questions may be added or substituted at the teacher's discretion. The lesson may be modeled differently or adjusted according to the current achievement level of the class. Allow enough time for student's covert thinking between questions or steps ( — ).

## MODELING (writer):

I am the writer for this map, and I have to write directions so other people can follow them on this map. Here is a list of special information about the map. It tells about some hazards and other conditions that are not shown on the large map. The little map has numbers that correspond with this information and show where these things are located. I will read the information carefully and mark anything relevant on the large map. Now I'll look at the map and locate the starting point. — I see it. I also have to find the goal. — There it is.

Next, I need to use the special information to find a usable path that will get me from the starting point to the goal. If the path forks or turns, I will have to choose which way to go. — I will follow each possible path to see if I can really get through. — If there is something in the way, I will have to go around the obstacle by selecting a different path. — If the special information tells me to complete a task enroute, I must select a path that will get me to that spot on the map.

Then I will need to describe the particular path I have chosen so anyone reading these directions will not get lost. As I write my directions, I have to remember to ask myself specific questions, such as: Which way am I facing? — In what direction does the path lie? — As I go by an object, I have to remember to ask: What is it? — What does it look like? — Where is it located? — How can I describe it so the reader will know I am talking about this one and not another one that looks almost the same? — What is special about this one? — How is it different from the other? — What is it near? — Does it face a certain direction? — I must remember to use words like *around, through, near, under, over,* and *behind* to describe where the path is leading. — Are there any other words I might need to use?

Now, let's check to see if my directions are complete. I will begin at the starting place and see if my directions will lead me to the goal. Did I note everything I passed? — Did I describe the direction correctly? — Did I provide enough important indicators or landmarks to guide the reader? — Did I use the best words to describe everything? — What other words might I use to make my directions more precise? — Do my sentences make sense? — Do I need to add or change anything? — Are my sentences in a logical order? — Where should I make changes so one thing follows another in the right sequence? — Do my directions really say what I want them to say? — Will someone else be able to read, understand, and follow these directions? —

## MODELING (reader):

Here I have some directions that someone else has written for me. I am using the same large map, but the writer had different special information than I, so these directions will not be the same as those I wrote. I will be trying to follow a route different from the one I drew on the map.

I have to read these directions and follow them on the map to reach the goal. — If the starting point and goal are not marked on the map, the directions will tell me where they are located. — I have to read very carefully and think about each step as I go along. — I have to check directions and look for certain landmarks or indicators. — I have to determine which object on the map is the one being described. — This object looks like it, but so does this one. — I wonder which is the correct one? — I had better read the description again so I can compare and contrast all of these items that look alike. — I also have to follow each step in order or I could get lost or miss finding the goal. — The path goes off in many directions here. Maybe I could go this way. It would be shorter. — Let's see what the directions say. No, I cannot go that way because there is an obstacle in the path. — I'll have to choose another route. How about this one? — The directions say this would be the best way. What is next? — I am supposed to go to this spot and find the goal. Good! I found it! — Finally, I will check my route one more time against the written directions to be certain I followed the route described.

## DIRECTIONS FOR GUIDED COOPERATIVE PRACTICE:

Each activity includes a large map plus two separate Writer's Information boxes. The information refers to special conditions not indicated on the large map. The boxes also include a much smaller map with markings showing the location of each special condition.

Select one of the activities. Divide the class into groups of four, then into pairs within each group. Distribute one copy of the large map to each student. Cut the Writer's Information sheets in half and give one section to each pair in a group. Ask the pairs to set aside one copy of the large map to use in the latter part of the activity.

Each pair should then study their specific Writer's Information and their large and small maps. Working as a team, they should mark the special information on the large map and then select and draw a safe route from START to GOAL. (The more advanced map activities require the students to identify the starting point and the goal from the Writer's Information.) After drawing in their route, each pair then develops written instructions for following their selected route. These instructions should include an accurate and complete description of the route with explanations for choosing or avoiding a particular path. When they have finished, each member of the pair should check the written instructions against the map and Writer's Information for errors or omissions.

                    © 1989 MIDWEST PUBLICATIONS • P.O. Box 448, Pacific Grove, CA  93950

Pairs in each group should then exchange **only** the sheet containing their written instructions. **No marked maps or Writer's Information sheets should change hands.** Still working cooperatively, students are to read the instructions and directions provided by the other pair. They are to apply the information to their **unmarked** map and indicate the route described. Before returning the completed map to the writers for confirmation, each student in the cooperative pair should check the indicated route against the written directions for errors or omissions.

Use as many of these activities as needed to make the students feel comfortable about solving these kinds of problems. Since they are supplemental activities, and since thorough discussion is essential, it is recommended that students do no more than one activity per day.

## EVALUATION:

Students will learn more and retain concepts in greater depth if they can develop and perfect these skills cooperatively with their classmates in an open-learning environment.

Did they find the goal? Did they find the best and quickest way to the goal? Did they write clear directions? Define and discuss each problem area. Students can learn from their mistakes when free to evaluate them in a nonthreatening setting. Encourage them to explore the reasons for their errors, the consequences of those errors, and ways to correct and improve their thinking processes.

Allow plenty of time for discussion of successful strategies as well. Include exchanging information about what has been learned and how useful these activities can be when applied to other lessons, other disciplines, and to the students' environments outside of school. By actively sharing problems and possible solutions, students will learn from each other as they progress through the activities.

## EXTENDING ACTIVITIES:

Additional copies of the large maps can be made so students can create their own scenarios and Writer's Information for plotting new routes and writing new descriptions.

Students may also wish to create their own maps for completely new activities.

## PICNIC!
### Writer's Information

Direct your reader from the starting point to the goal. You have the following knowledge that is not available on the reader's map. Mark your copy of the map, then create and describe a path to the goal.

1  Walking on the grass is not permitted anywhere in the park except in the picnic area (GOAL).

2  You can see a statue of a lion and a tennis court from this path.

3  A skateboard contest is taking place here. The cement path surrounding the area is closed for observers and contestants.

4  This walkway is closed today because of migrating caterpillars.

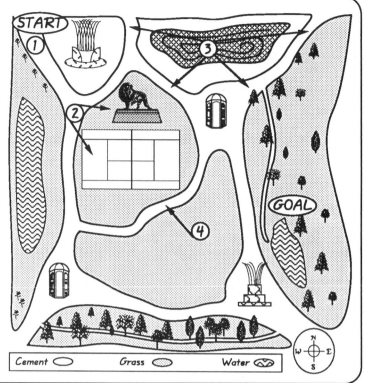

## Sample Directions for the Reader

As you enter the park at the northwest entrance, on your right you will see a grassy area with flowers along the walkway. You may not walk on the grass anywhere in this park except in the picnic area. On your left is a cement area with a circular cement fountain. The path that goes to the left around the fountain is closed today for a skateboard contest.

If you look straight ahead, you should be able to see a statue of a lion and a tennis court. Take the path that leads past them. There should be a large lake on your right. After you pass the tennis court, you will see a cement path on your left. This path is closed because of migrating caterpillars. Just after you pass the path, you should see a gazebo (a small building with a rounded roof and open panels or sides). Go to the gazebo and follow the path that goes toward the left (east). There will be a grassy area on your left and a grassy area with trees on your right.

When you reach a three-tiered rock fountain, turn left (north) and walk up the cement path just past a small lake or pond on your right. Just beyond the pond, turn right off the path. You should then see the picnic area where the birthday party is being held straight ahead of you.

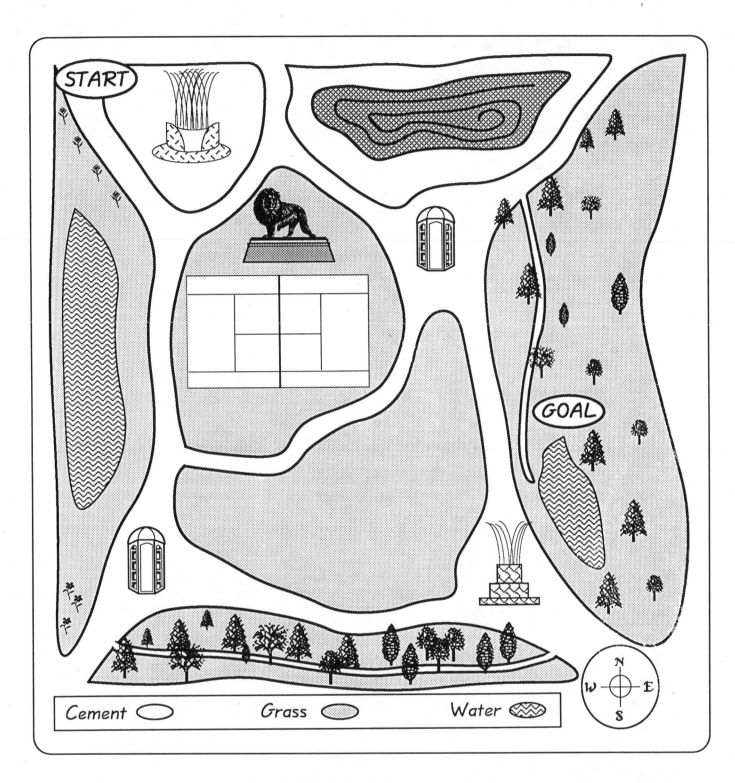

## PICNIC!

You have been invited to a picnic birthday party taking place in a park in your city. This map of the park was sent with your invitation, but you will need additional directions to find the party. You are to meet a friend at the northwest entrance to the park, and the friend will give you written directions for finding the party.

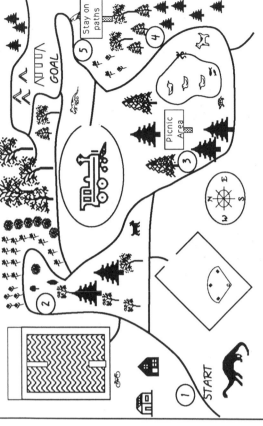

## PARK-ABOUTS • 2
### Writer Information

Direct your reader from the starting point to the GOAL. You have the following knowledge that is not available on the reader's map. Mark your copy of the map, then create and describe a path to the goal.

1. You must stay on the paths to protect the spring grass plantings except in the picnic, playground, and locomotive areas.

2. Path closed because an eagle is nesting in a nearby tree.

3. This area and the nearby path are closed due to a large family-reunion picnic.

4. This area has many mosquitos from the duck pond. Stay away unless you want to get bitten.

5. This path is being resurfaced here.

## PARK-ABOUTS • 1
### Writer Information

Direct your reader from the starting point to the GOAL. You have the following knowledge that is not available on the reader's map. Mark your copy of the map, then create and describe a path to the goal.

1. You must stay on the paths to protect the spring grass plantings except in the picnic, playground, and locomotive areas.

2. This path ends here.

3. Path closed. Salamanders are migrating.

4. Path closed due to wasp nests in trees.

5. Path is under construction here.

© 1989 MIDWEST PUBLICATIONS • P.O. Box 448, Pacific Grove, CA 93950

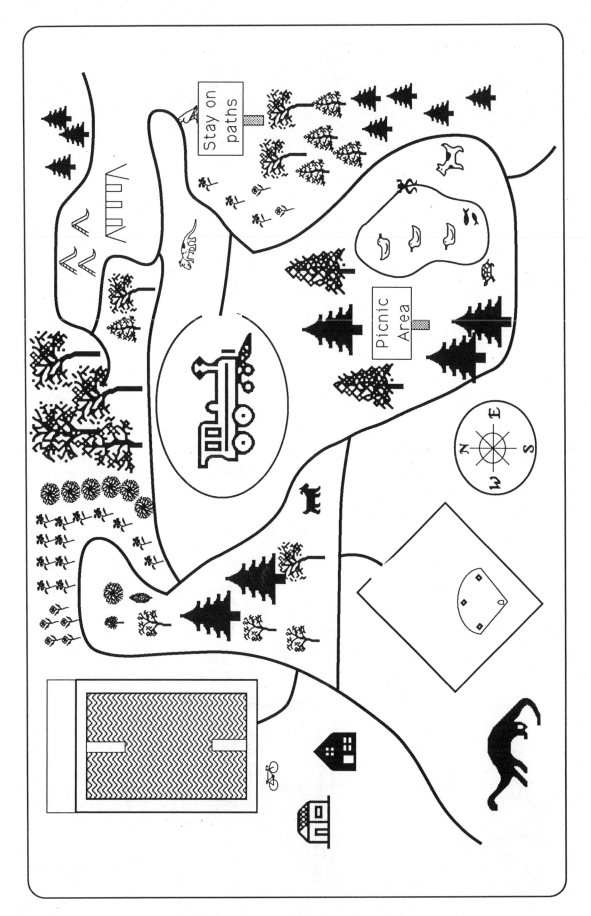

## PARK-ABOUTS

You are planning to spend Saturday at the city park. The park has a large swimming pool, a locomotive to play on, an ongoing baseball game, and other wonderful things to do and see. You have a map of the park, but because there has been construction taking place and because there are often unexpected happenings, you will have to ask for more detailed directions from one of the park guides.

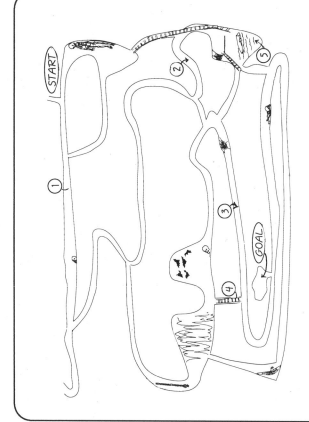

## SPELUNKING • 2
### Writer Information

Direct your reader from the starting point to the GOAL (the lost children). You have the following knowledge that is not available on the reader's map. Mark your copy of the map, then create and describe a path to the goal.

1. The passage at this point has been filled with dirt that has fallen through the mouth of the cave.

2. A huge, deep hole has formed here in the cave floor. You cannot get through safely.

3. A cave-in here has completely blocked this passageway.

4. The rungs on this ladder have rotted and fallen off.

5. High water in this cavern makes it impossible to get through at this point.

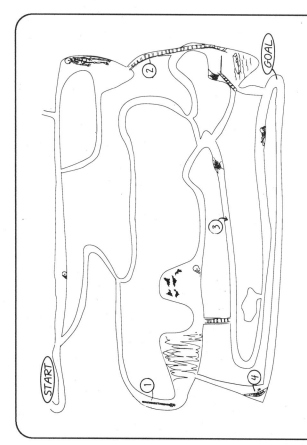

## SPELUNKING • 1
### Writer Information

Direct your reader from the starting point to the GOAL (the lost children). You have the following knowledge that is not available on the reader's map. Mark your copy of the map, then create and describe a path to the goal.

1. The rope you need to get down safely into the next level of the caves is broken.

2. A rock has rolled down and filled the cave so no one can get through here.

3. A cave-in here has completely blocked this passageway.

4. This is a poison spider area. Do not try to take this route.

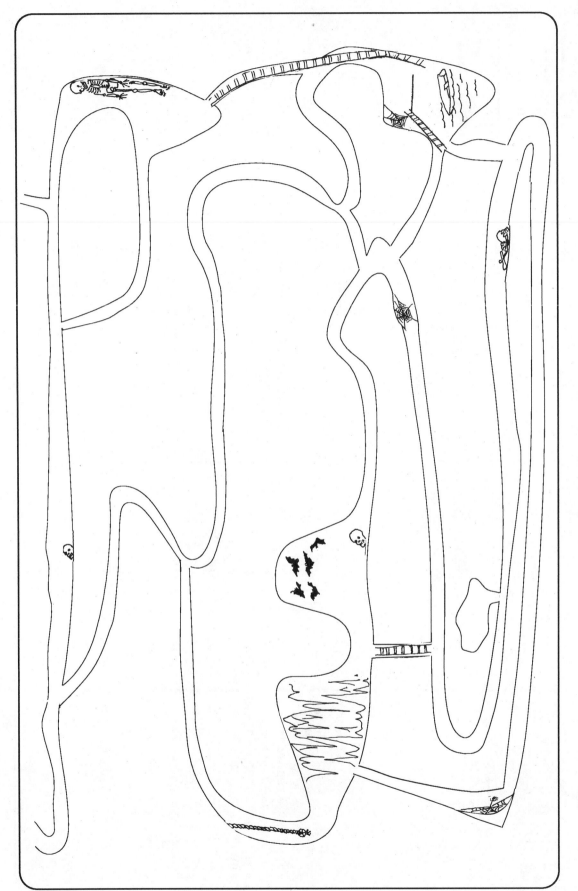

## SPELUNKING

Your brother and sister are lost in the Mystery Caves. Your search party has come to find them. No one has been in the caves in years. They are dark and full of bats, cobwebs, pools of water, and old skulls and bones. You have a map, but only an old prospector knows the caves well enough to direct you and the other searchers. The prospector's directions include important information that is not on your printed map.

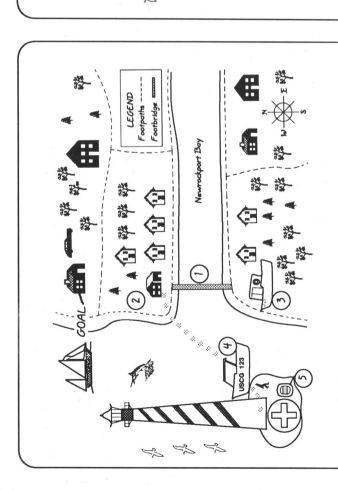

## SMUGGLERS AHOY • 2
### Writer Information

Direct your reader from the starting point to the GOAL. You have the following knowledge that is not available on the reader's map. Mark your copy of the map, then create and describe a path to the goal.

1  Smuggler lookout posted here.

2  Abandoned house. You can get to the hidden underwater tunnel by going down into the basement.

3  The bridge is under construction and cannot be used.

4  This path ends here.

5  This path is unlighted at night.

6  This road goes directly south.

## SMUGGLERS AHOY • 1
### Writer Information

Direct your reader from the starting point to the GOAL. You have the following knowledge that is not available on the reader's map. Mark your copy of the map, then create and describe a path to the goal.

1  Low bridge. Only enough clearance for rowboats and rafts.

2  Smugglers have a lookout at this point.

3  The boat is seaworthy and full of fuel.

4  The Coast Guard boat is out of fuel.

5  The raft is usable very close to shore and in the bay.

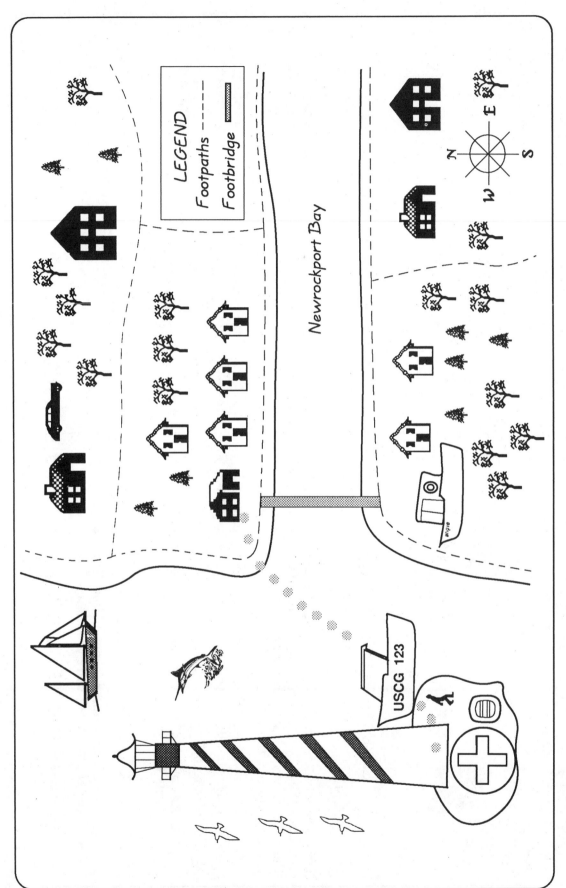

## SMUGGLERS AHOY!

You are the Coast Guard skipper of a small boat that checks the automatic lighthouses along the coast. In the process of servicing the one at Newrockport Bay, you see the smugglers' schooner whose crew has avoided capture for months. The smugglers have been posing as sailing people, unloading their art treasures at night and hiding them. With no time to seek help, you and your crew set out to capture them. An old sea captain who knows Newrockport well will give you additional directions for finding the treasures and capturing the smugglers.

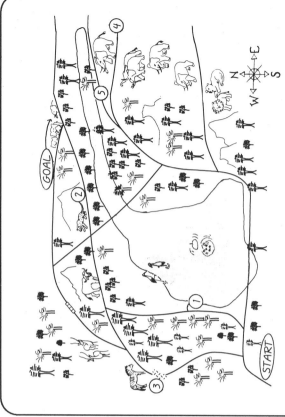

## SAVE THE ELEPHANTS • 2
### Writer Information

Direct your reader from the starting point to the GOAL. You have the following knowledge that is not available on the reader's map. Mark your copy of the map, then create and describe a path to the goal.

1  A large hippo considers this his territory. He is very protective—and quite dangerous.

2  A lioness (with cubs) has recently attacked others who have walked on this path.

3  Crocodiles in abundance inhabit this marshy area.

4  This road goes directly east.

5  This road has been flooded out by heavy spring rains.

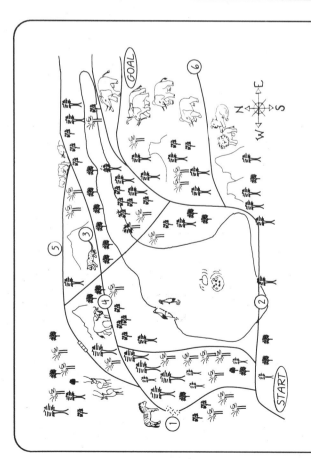

## SAVE THE ELEPHANTS • 1
### Writer Information

Direct your reader from the starting point to the GOAL. You have the following knowledge that is not available on the reader's map. Mark your copy of the map, then create and describe a path to the goal.

1  A portion of this road has turned into quicksand due to water seepage.

2  The bridge here is out.

3  An injured leopard has attacked people along this road.

4  The presence of a water buffalo in this area makes walking on this road unsafe.

5  The road is under construction here. Both car and foot traffic are prohibited.

6  This road turns south at this point.

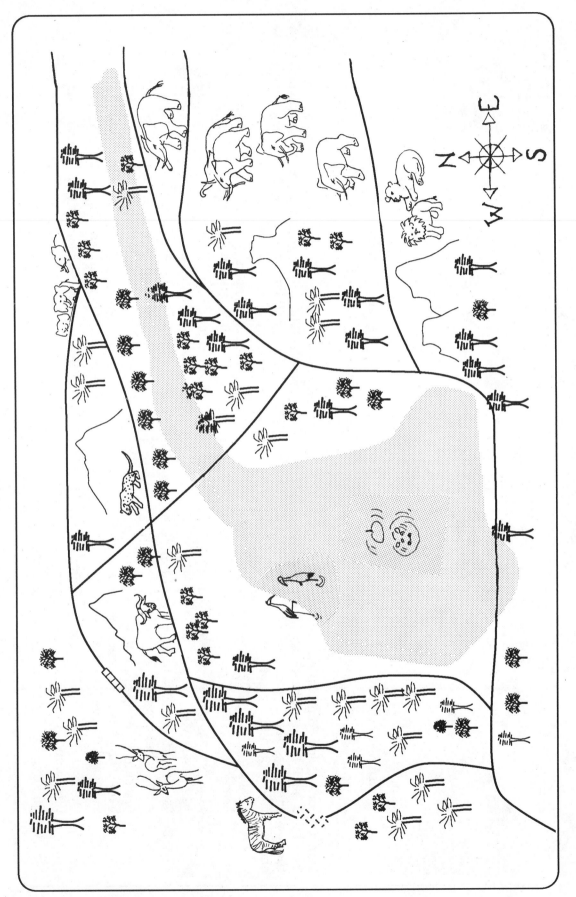

## SAVE THE ELEPHANTS

You are a park ranger on a large game preserve in Africa. Your particular responsibility is the elephants. Ivory poachers have been killing elephants for their tusks, often leaving baby elephants on their own. You have to travel from your station to the edge of the jungle to reach the elephants. However, because rains have made roads impassable, you have to travel on foot. It is unsafe to leave the roads because of jungle hazards and dense growth. You will need to get more information on road and trail conditions from the patrol department.

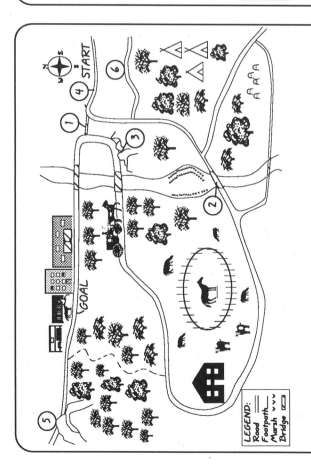

## MARSHAL AND OUTLAWS • 2
### Writer Information

Direct your reader from the starting point to the GOAL. You have the following knowledge that is not available on the reader's map. Mark your copy of the map, then create and describe a path to the goal.

1  Indians who are unfriendly guard the road at these points.

2  Boulders have rolled down on this path, making it impossible to get through.

3  It would be dangerous to leave the road or footpaths because numerous outlaws are scattered throughout the area.

4  Cattle are being driven east on this road. Individual riders cannot get through.

5  This road was washed out in a flash flood.

## MARSHAL AND OUTLAWS • 1
### Writer Information

Direct your reader from the starting point to the GOAL. You have the following knowledge that is not available on the reader's map. Mark your copy of the map, then create and describe a path to the goal.

1  The suspension bridge over the gully has been cut down.

2  This bridge was washed out in last winter's floods.

3  Three outlaw lookouts are guarding the road at this point.

4  It would be dangerous to leave the road or footpaths because numerous outlaws are scattered throughout the area.

5  Outlaws keep a watch on the town from this point.

6  This road was dynamited by prospectors.

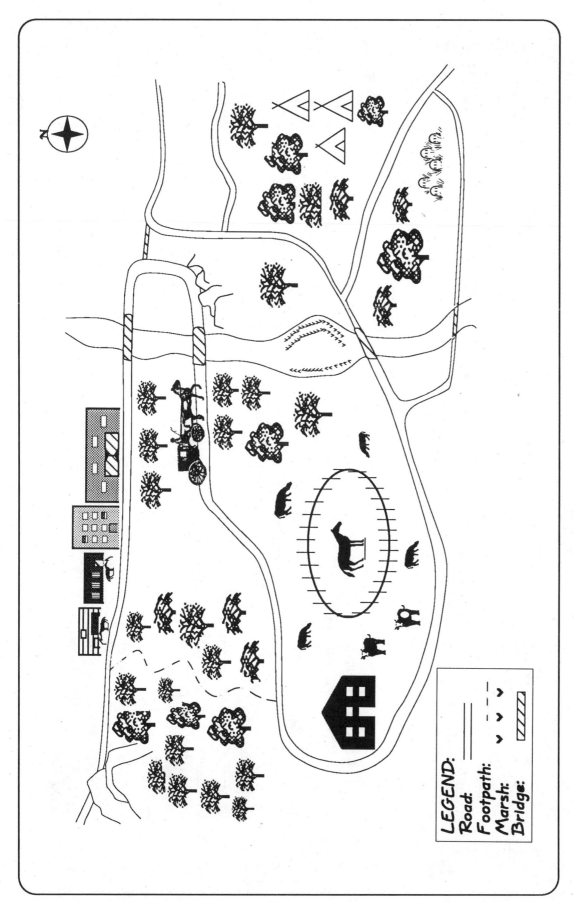

## MARSHAL AND OUTLAWS

Sidewinder Gulch has been attacked by outlaws. You, as U.S. Marshal, and your posse have been sent to capture them. You have a map (above), but only the guide to the Indian territory, Frenchy, knows the special information necessary for finding them without endangering yourself or the posse. These directions include important information that is not on your printed map.

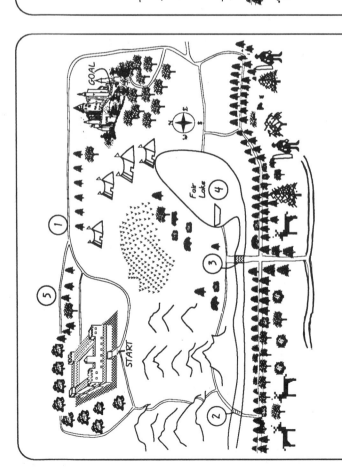

## KNIGHTS OF OLD • 2
### Writer Information

Direct your reader from the starting point to the GOAL. You have the following knowledge that is not available on the reader's map. Mark your copy of the map, then create and describe a path to the goal.

1 A rock slide blocks the road at this point.

2 This bridge is in enemy hands.

3 A dragon has made a lair above this road. He grabs people and locks them in his lair.

4 For safety reasons, you must stay on the roads.

5 Enemy soldiers have been keeping this road under guard.

6 The path on this side of the lake is visible to soldiers in the enemy camp.

## KNIGHTS OF OLD • 1
### Writer Information

Direct your reader from the starting point to the GOAL. You have the following knowledge that is not available on the reader's map. Mark your copy of the map, then create and describe a path to the goal.

1 Sir Mirfan's men guard this road.

2 A dangerous troll family lives under this bridge. They eat people and crunch their bones with relish.

3 This bridge has been washed out.

4 A marshy area surrounds the lake. It is dangerous to go around the lake. Note the small boat here.

5 For safety reasons, you must stay on the marked roads.

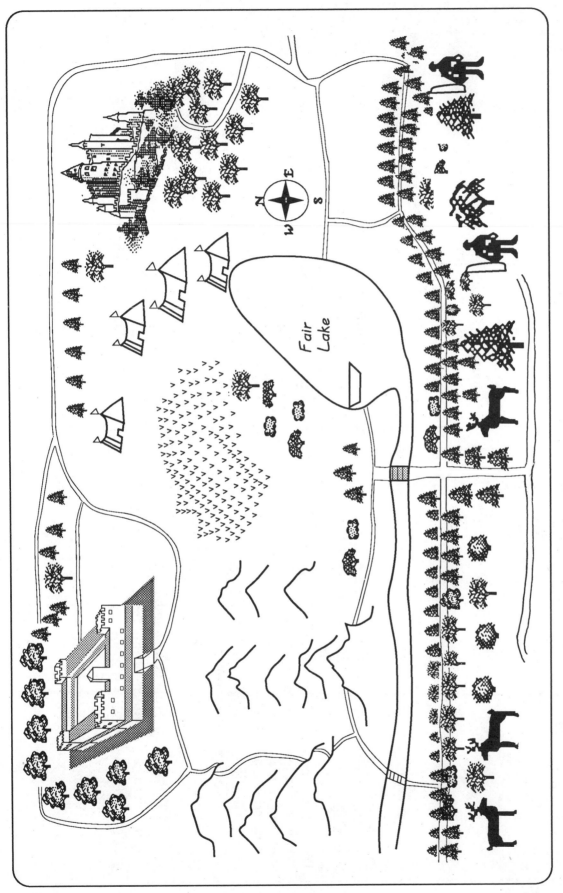

## KNIGHTS OF OLD

You, Sir Bold, discover that soldiers from the evil knight, Sir Mirfan, have pitched tents and are preparing to capture Lady Sylvia, who has agreed to marry you and who lives in a nearby castle. Sir Mirfan also has poachers in the forest killing your game to feed his troops. You have a map (above), but only the page, John, who has escaped from Sir Mirfan's soldiers to join you, can give you the specific information necessary to reach the destinations safely. These directions include important information that is not on your printed map.

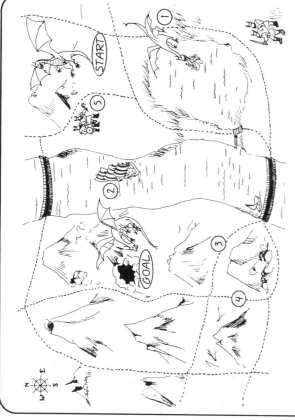

## VIKINGS AND DRAGONS • 2
### Writer Information

Direct your reader from the starting point to the GOAL. You have the following knowledge that is not available on the reader's map. Mark your copy of the map, then create and describe a path to the goal.

1  A dragon, Naoj, guards this trail.

2  Viking ships make the river unsafe here.

3  Snow has closed this mountain pass.

4  A dangerous mountain tribe has men stationed here.

5  Vikings are camped along this route. They have lookouts guarding this road.

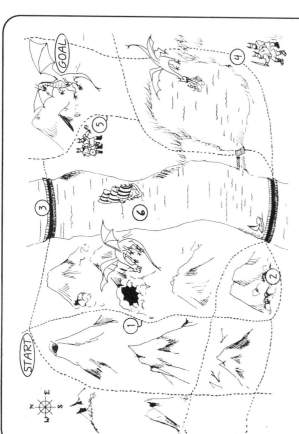

## VIKINGS AND DRAGONS • 1
### Writer Information

Direct your reader from the starting point to the GOAL. You have the following knowledge that is not available on the reader's map. Mark your copy of the map, then create and describe a path to the goal.

1  Sutrebla, a dragon, has a lair above the trail. He is dangerous.

2  An avalanche at this point makes the trail impossible to pass.

3  This bridge is in Viking hands.

4  Vikings are guarding this trail.

5  There are Viking soldiers camped on this road.

6  Viking ships make it impossible to pass this point on the river.

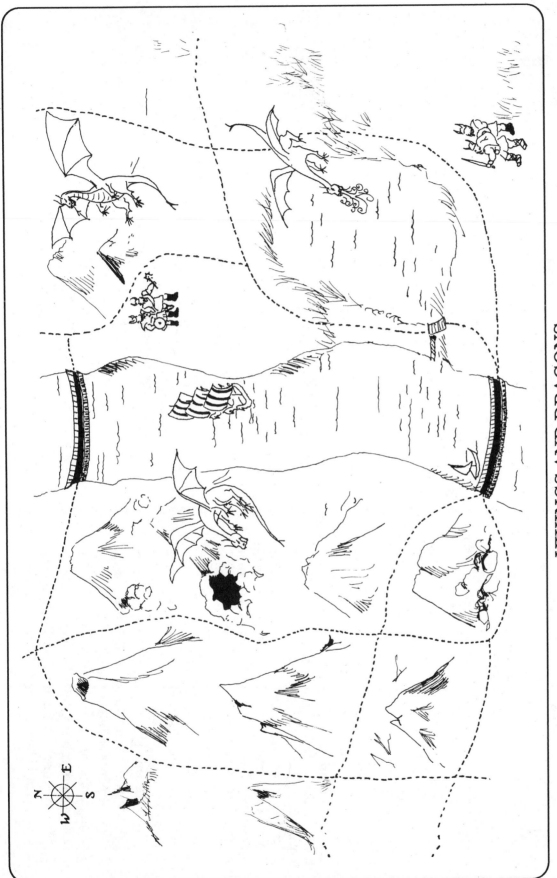

## VIKINGS AND DRAGONS

Nerak, a dragon, has stolen the royal jewels and hidden them in his lair. You, Sir Gavin, are assigned by the king to recapture them from the dragon before the Vikings seize them. The Vikings have been waging war against your kingdom so you must secretly pass by them. Also, the Vikings have been bribing the dragons to do battle on their side against your king and kingdom. The gnome, Jeremy, knows the dragon country well and will give you special instructions so you can safely complete your assignment.

## VISIT TO THE WETLANDS • 2
### Writer Information

While you are visiting your aunt and uncle in the wetlands, Cousin Mae would like you to come spend the day fishing. Pay very close attention to these special instructions so you get there safely.

1 Aunt and Uncle's cabin is behind the Old Lone Tree.
2 Save fuel by going with current toward this spot.
3 Fill up with gas at Gilly's. He closes at noon.
4 Save time by portaging boat across sand spit. Vipers live around the tree.
5 Pick up bait.
6 Thick mist in this reed bed. Water is very shallow.
7 Posted panther area. Protected by Fish and Game officers. Violators arrested.
8 Water here full of snags.
9 Dangerous type characters live here.
10 My house is southeast of the sunken cabin. Lunch will be waiting.

## VISIT TO THE WETLANDS • 1
### Writer Information

You have been invited to visit relatives at their cabin way back in the wetlands along the coast. You take an early morning flight and then ride a bus to Crab's Landing. Your relatives will leave a map and note for you there. "Sorry can't meet you. Read map and notes carefully. Leave now. Essential you get to cabin before dark."

1 Boat left for you at Marsh's Dock.
2 Swift currents can be a problem. Current beyond muskrat houses is sluggish.
3 Thick mist in this reed bed. Danger of getting lost and very shallow water.
4 Steer for this point. Water is deep and calm.
5 Many aggressive alligators live around here.
6 Posted panther release area.
7 Dangerous characters live here.
8 Snags here can rip the bottom of the boat.
9 Stop for lunch at Fudd's Fish Restaurant.
10 Our cabin is behind the Old Lone Tree.

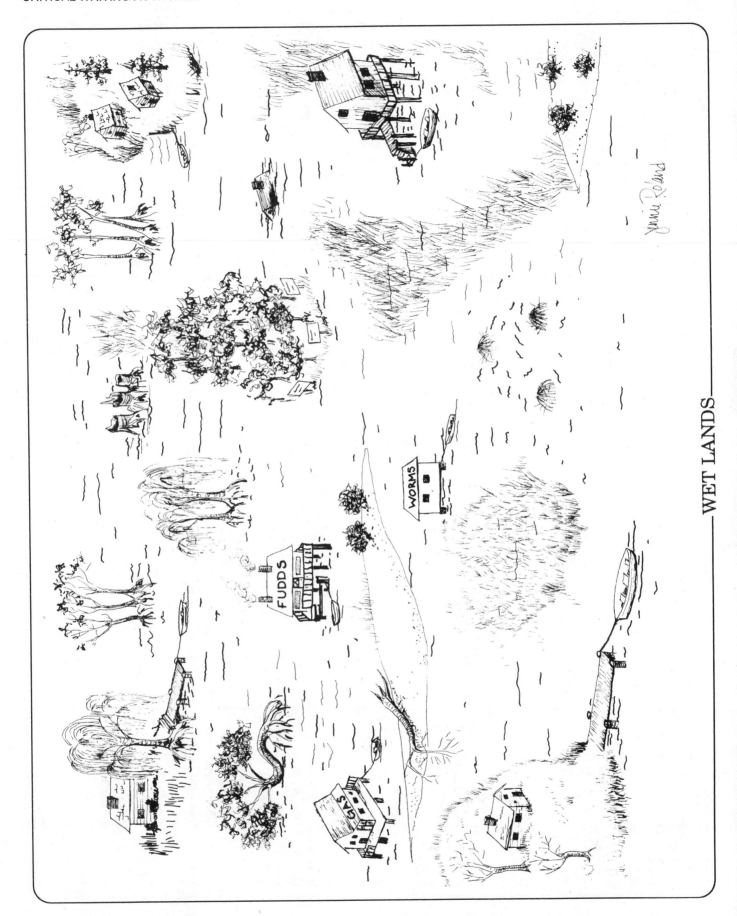

WET LANDS

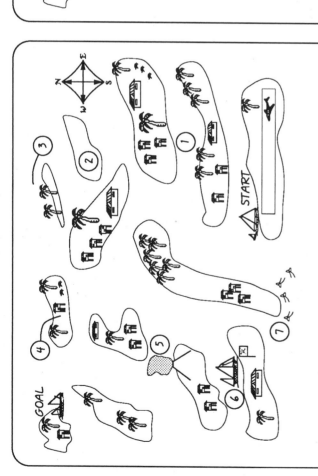

## ISLAND ADVENTURES • 2
### Writer Information

Direct your reader from the starting point to the GOAL. You have the following knowledge that is not available on the reader's map. Mark your copy of the map, then create and describe a path to the goal.

1. The waters here have many great white sharks. Winds that could capsize a boat make it unsafe to sail nearby.

2. High winds are hitting the island's east side.

3. Islanders with poison blowguns guard this passage.

4. Whales are nearby. Do not disturb them.

5. A coral reef makes the water too shallow for the boat.

6. Ships are forbidden in this turtle nesting area.

7. Low tide has closed this passage.

## ISLAND ADVENTURES • 1
### Writer Information

Direct your reader from the starting point to the GOAL. You have the following knowledge that is not available on the reader's map. Mark your copy of the map, then create and describe a path to the goal.

1. There is a shallow reef here. Danger!

2. This island and nearby water are still unsafe from nuclear testing 20 years ago.

3. Gale winds make this passage unsafe.

4. Cannibals with boats live here and patrol all surrounding waterways.

5. An active volcano is throwing out lava.

6. Island pirates make this area unsafe.

7. Whales are summering here. Do not disturb them!

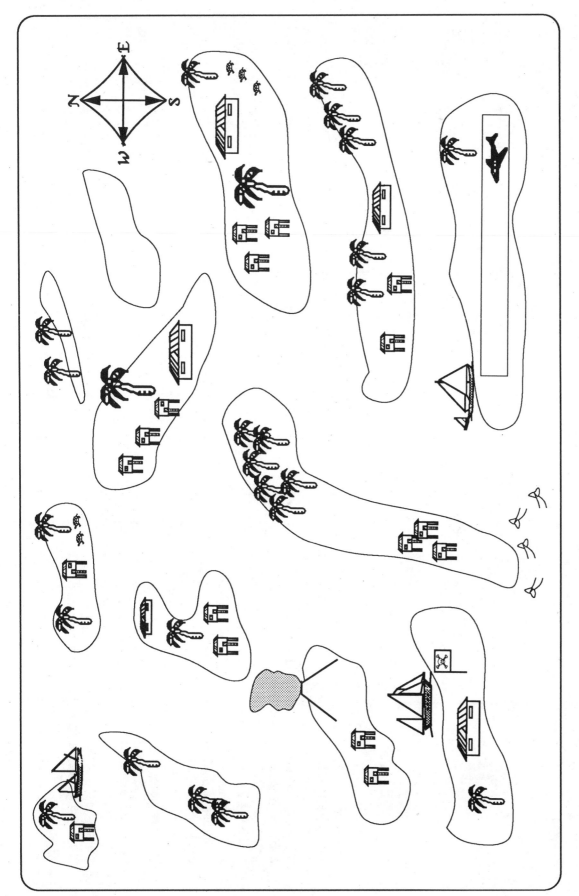

## ISLAND ADVENTURES

You, a journalist, are arriving by plane in the Danger Islands. Your assignment will be given at the airstrip. The only way to reach the destination is by ship. Because of the high winds and rough ocean, the ship cannot sail safely outside the map's limits. Your map is not complete. You must rely on the island guide who knows how to reach the destination safely. His directions include important information that is not on your printed map.

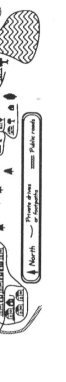

## GOING TO THE ZOO • 2
### Writer Information

Direct your reader from the starting point to the goal. You have the following knowledge that is not available on the reader's map. Mark your copy of the map, then create and describe a path to the goal.

1. Your friend is walking to your father's office and may travel only on indicated footpaths or along the shoulders of safe highways.

2. A footbridge over the highway at this point connects with the footpaths on either side.

3. Celebrities attending a local golf tournament here have attracted such a crowd of spectators that no one can walk anywhere in the park today.

4. No pedestrians are allowed on this highway.

5. A new walking path has just opened along the shoulder of this road from here south to the footpath.

6. An unmarked path turns off here and goes to the back door of your father's office building.

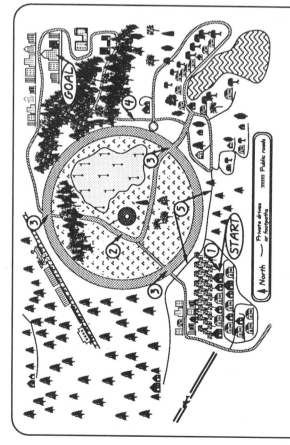

## GOING TO THE ZOO • 1
### Writer Information

Direct your reader from the starting point to the goal. You have the following knowledge that is not available on the reader's map. Mark your copy of the map, then create and describe a path to the goal.

1. Since it is very cold outside, your friend will be driven to your father's office. Give directions for getting there by car on public roads.

2. This road is closed. Several large trees were knocked across it during a severe ice storm last night.

3. This is a 4-way intersection with a stop light that allows drivers to go left, right, or straight ahead.

4. A truck driver lost control of her truck in the ice storm and turned over at this point. No one was hurt, but the road is closed to all traffic until the wreckage is cleared. Since you do not know when that will be, direct your friend to avoid this spot.

5. This is a foot path, not a private drive.

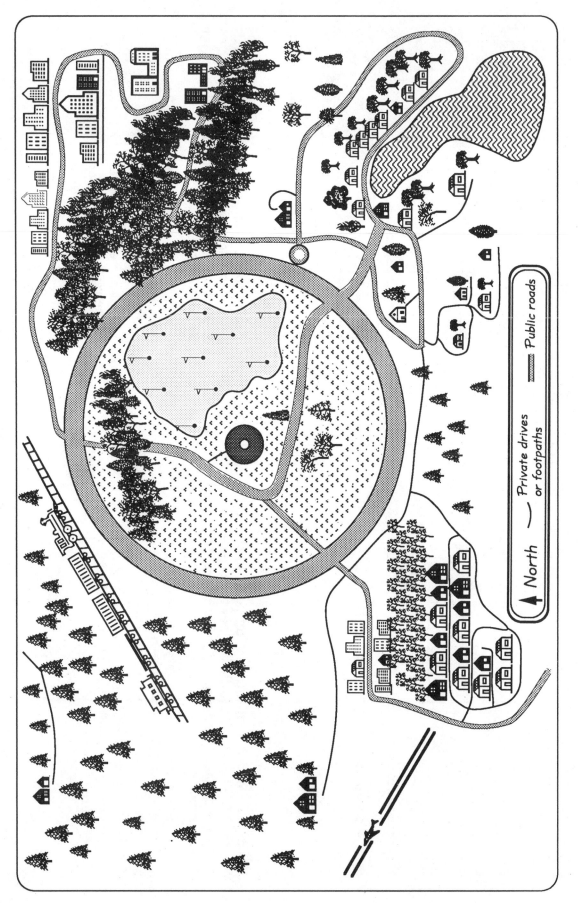

## GOING TO THE ZOO

You are spending your spring break with your grandparents, and a friend has invited you to join his family for a trip to the zoo today. Your friend will give you written directions to his father's office building, where you are to meet them. These directions include important local information that is not on the map you have. Depending on how far it is, you might either walk to the office or be driven by your grandfather.

North

— Private drives or footpaths

Public roads

© 1989 MIDWEST PUBLICATIONS • P.O. Box 448, Pacific Grove, CA 93950

## BUSING IT • 2
### Writer Information

Direct your reader from the starting point to the GOAL. You have the following knowledge that is not available on the reader's map. Mark your copy of the map, then create and describe a path to the goal.

1   Each bus stops at every intersection. The bus stop nearest to your reader (where the reader has to board the bus) is here.

2   The bus stop nearest the doctor's office (where the reader should get off the bus) is here.

## BUSING IT • 1
### Writer Information

Direct your reader from the starting point to the GOAL. You have the following knowledge that is not available on the reader's map. Mark your copy of the map, then create and describe a path to the goal.

1   Each bus stops at every intersection. The bus stop nearest to your reader (where the reader has to board the bus) is here.

2   The bus stop nearest the doctor's office (where the reader should get off the bus) is here.

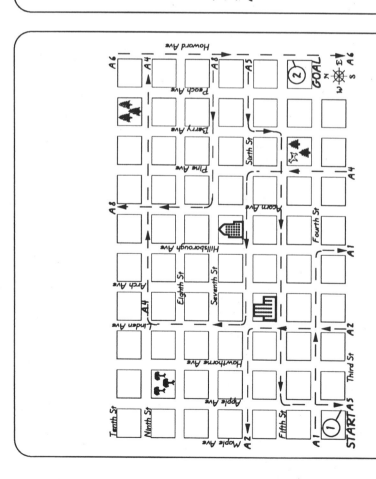

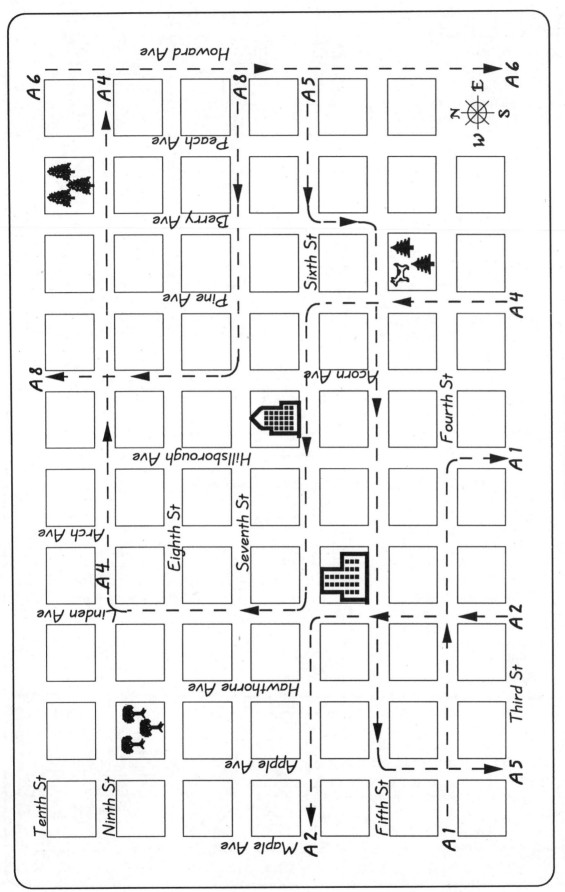

## BUSING IT

You have sprained your ankle in sports and you need a cane to walk. To get to the doctor, you have to use the buses. On the map, the bus routes are shown by dotted lines. The different route numbers are shown by a letter and a number, for example, A4, A8, and so on. The ar- rows show the direction the bus travels. Some buses do not travel just on one street, but may turn and go on other streets. You have this map, but you will need additional information from the bus driver to reach your destination.

## THE OLD SWIMMING HOLE • 1
### Writer Information

Direct your reader from the starting point to the goal. You have the following knowledge that is not available on the reader's map. Mark your copy of the map, then create and describe a path to the goal.

1  All fences except these are climbable.

2  They are filling the silo today. People not involved in the task are to stay out of this area because of the heavy machinery.

3  Several new head of cattle have recently been put into this pasture. Since some of them might not be too friendly, everyone is to stay out of the field.

4  Now that most of the vegetables have been harvested, Grandmother has turned the chickens loose in her backyard and garden. No one can open the gates or walk through this area while the chickens are loose.

5  They are blasting here today. Everyone is to stay away.

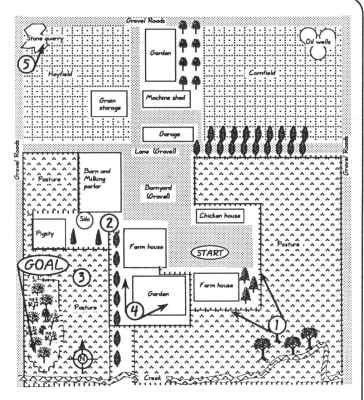

## THE OLD SWIMMING HOLE • 2
### Writer Information

Direct your reader from the starting point to the goal. You have the following knowledge that is not available on the reader's map. Mark your copy of the map, then create and describe a path to the goal.

1  All fences except these are climbable.

2  Your grandmother and mother are here planting fall vegetables. If you go past, you will be put to work and have to give up swimming for the day.

3  Cows from this pasture will be going out the gate here and up the lane when you want to go to the swimming hole.

4  The milk cows come up the lane and into the barn at this point. No one can cross the lane while the cows are walking up it, for they are easily scared.

5  Trucks are hauling from here today. Stay clear of the area.

6  Stay away from this boundary. Recent flooding has made several dangerous sink holes appear.

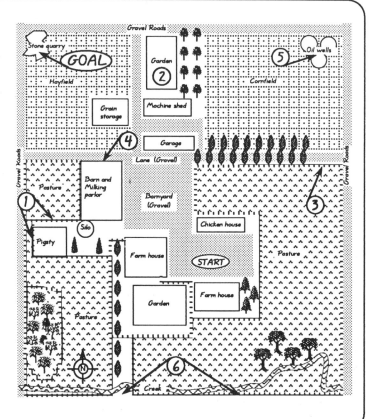

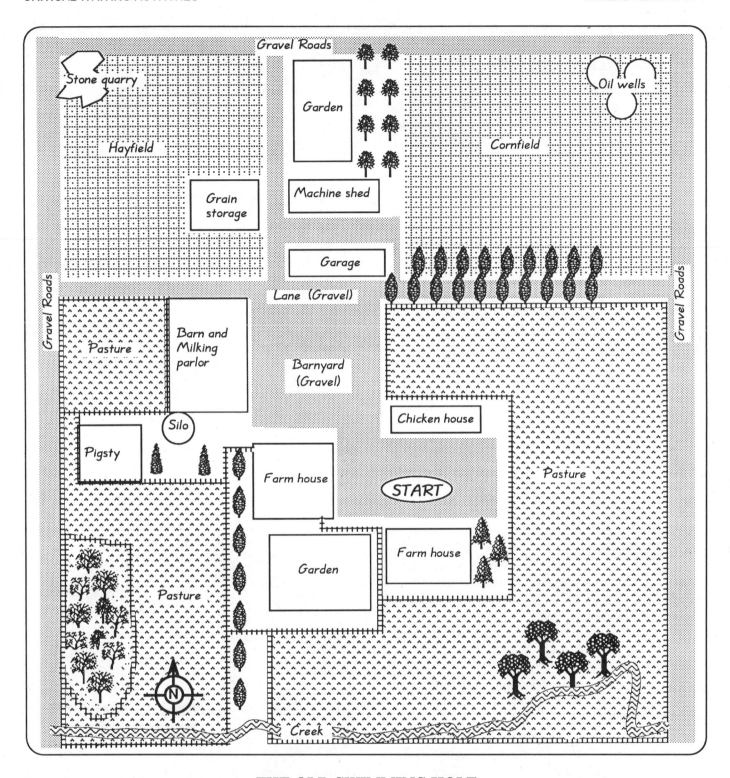

## THE OLD SWIMMING HOLE

The weather is hot and humid, and you have only three days left of your summer vacation on your uncle's farm. As a matter of fact, your cousins have started back to school already. All is not lost, however, for you have just gotten a telephone call from your cousins asking you to meet them at the swimming hole after school. You have a farm map, but the swimming hole is not shown on it. Your cousins will have to give you directions.

## WORLDS OF THRILLS • 1
### Writer Information

Direct your reader from the starting point to the goal. You have the following knowledge that is not available on the map. Mark your copy of the map, then create and describe a path to the goal.

1 This telephone is out of order. Use the other one to call park information.

2 A ferry temporarily located behind this snack bar will take people to the restaurant and the gift shop on the center island.

3 This bridge is closed for repair.

4 Crowds here are enormous due to a new dolphin show that will be starting in approximately fifteen minutes.

5 All trains will be in the roundhouse for inspection until 3:00 p.m.

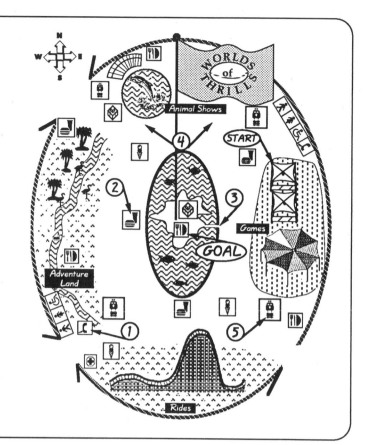

## WORLDS OF THRILLS • 2
### Writer Information

Direct your reader from the starting point to the goal. You have the following knowledge that is not available on the map. Mark your copy of the map, then create and describe a path to the goal.

1 There is a sign here that says, "Out of order. Please use a newly installed telephone near the Main Gate."

2 Main Gate area. The new telephone is behind the snack bar.

3 Since it is early in the season, the trains are not yet running and this is the only ice cream stand open. The crowd of people here is blocking through traffic.

4 A newly completed bridge here allows visitors to cut across the center of the park.

5 Extensive construction here has closed this section of the park to all except authorized personnel.

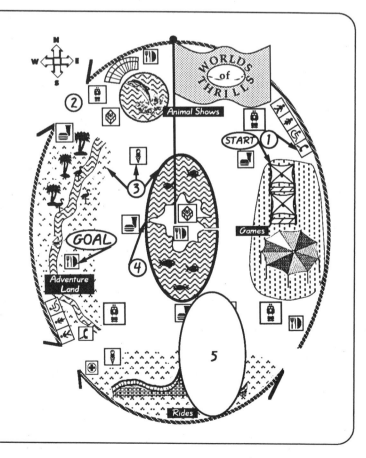

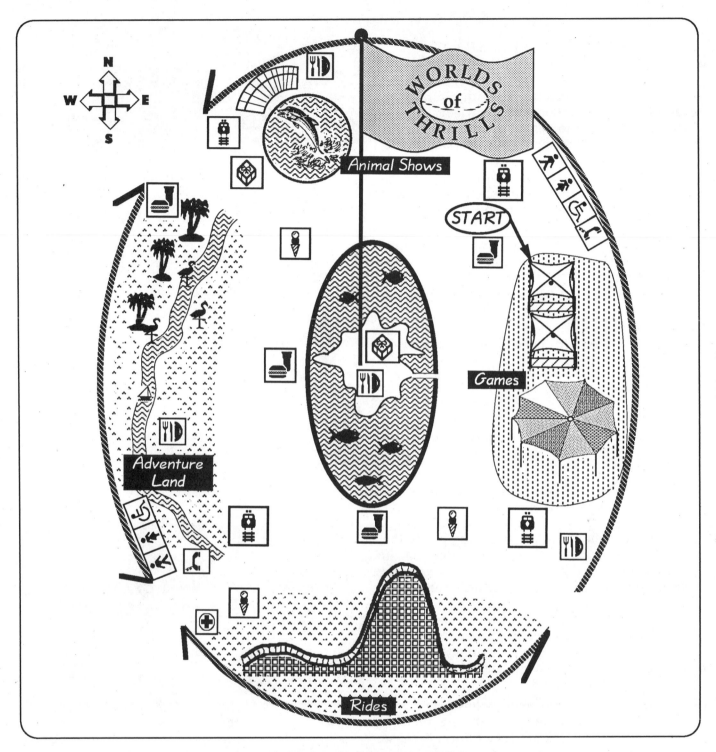

## WORLDS OF THRILLS

You've been having a great time at the "Worlds of Thrills" amusement park, but you are getting a little hungry and you've spent nearly all of your money. If you can meet your parents before they finish eating, they will probably buy lunch for you. Your mother told you they would eat at the Silver Vein Restaurant, but it isn't identified on your park map. Also, lots of people are in the park today and several areas are under construction. You will have to call information on a park telephone to find the quickest way to the restaurant.

## THE HAUNTED HOUSE • 1
### Writer Information

Direct your reader from the starting point to the goal. You have the following knowledge that is not available on the reader's map. Mark your copy of the map, then create and describe a path to the goal.

1. You are helping a friend find clues to the location of a rare, valuable book on this property. The first clue to finding the book is written here.
2. Another clue can be found here, but beware.
3. Find the third clue buried here. You'd better bring a bone.
4. The next clue can be found in here. Then get out fast.
5. The last clue is in here. Take this and go get the book where it's been hidden for years.

## THE HAUNTED HOUSE • 2
### Writer Information

Direct your reader from the starting point to the goal. You have the following knowledge that is not available on the reader's map. Mark your copy of the map, then create and describe a path to the goal.

1. You are helping a friend find clues to the location of a rare, valuable book on this property. The first clue to finding the book is under a rock on the bank here. Watch out for strange creatures.
2. Another clue can be found in here.
3. Take the boat and find the third clue under a floorboard in here. You'd better hurry because the boat is leaky.
4. The next clue can be found buried right under this particular place.
5. Get the last clue from a special pocket in the collar here. Be sure to bring a bone. Then dig for the book where it has been buried in the ground for years—and run for your life.

THE HAUNTED HOUSE

## FINDING THE PHARAOHS • 1
### Writer Information

Direct your reader from the starting point to the GOAL. You have the following knowledge that is not available on the reader's map. Mark your copy of the map, then create and describe a path to the goal that will take the traveler safely from one source of directions to the next.

1　It is dangerous to leave the caravan routes.

2　This is contaminated water (you need to find water for the camels).

3　Bandits are camped here. The route is dangerous.

4　This is a sacred shrine. No non-Egyptians are permitted in this area.

5　Hungry crocodiles live along the Nile banks. Beware!

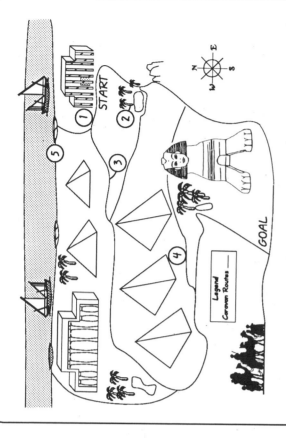

## FINDING THE PHARAOHS • 2
### Writer Information

Direct your reader from the starting point to the GOAL. You have the following knowledge that is not available on the reader's map. Mark your copy of the map, then create and describe a path to the goal that will take the traveler from one source of directions to the next.

1　It is dangerous to leave the caravan routes.

2　Hostile Hittite soldiers have captured this oasis from the Egyptians.

3　A sandstorm has closed this route.

4　Armed tomb robbers have been spotted in this area.

5　Boats may be used on the Nile.

34

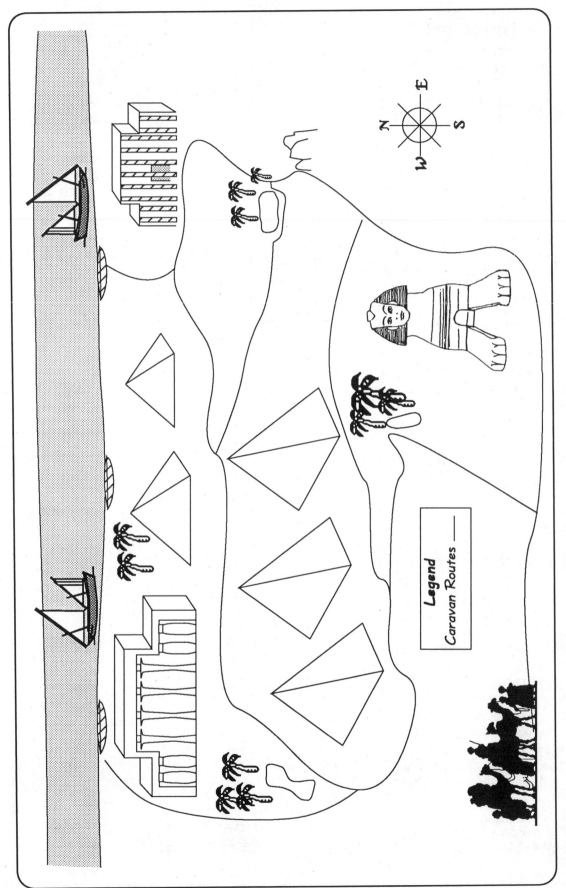

## FINDING THE PHARAOHS

It is the ninth year of the reign of King Akhenaton in Egypt. For the past three years you have been journeying in a caravan from the Euphrates Valley in search of someone rich and willing to exchange gold for your precious jewels. Finally, you arrive in Egypt, land of the fabulously rich Pharaohs. Since you only have an old map, you will need to consult a seer for current information about safe routes to and from the Pharaoh's palace.

**Legend**
*Caravan Routes* ―――

## BASEBALL CHAMPIONSHIP • 1
### Writer Information

Direct your reader from the starting point to the GOAL. You have the following facts that are not available on the reader's map. Mark your copy of the map, then create and describe a path to the goal.

1. A mud slide is blocking Big Sur Boulevard at this point. There is no through traffic.

2. The annual whale migration has created a terrible traffic jam from here to 5th Avenue.

3. The Atlantic Grove Marathon has closed Monterey Avenue to traffic today. The only open crossing is at this point.

4. Sand City is having a sandcastle contest on this beach today. Only the southbound lane of Bayview Boulevard is open.

5. North of this intersection, Forest Boulevard is one-way southbound. Northbound traffic must use Main Street.

6. This is the only entrance to the park. Everyone must enter here, then proceed to the ball field (GOAL).

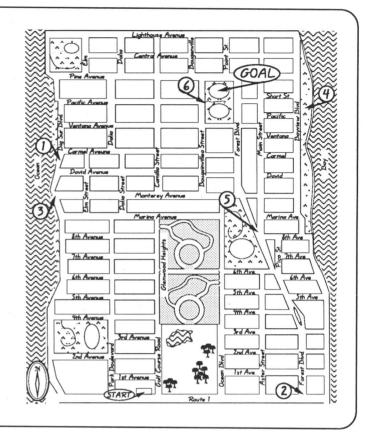

## BASEBALL CHAMPIONSHIP • 2
### Writer Information

Direct your reader from the starting point to the GOAL. You have the following facts that are not available on the reader's map. Mark your copy of the map, then create and describe a path to the goal.

1. For these two blocks, Elm is one-way northbound.

2. This street is entirely one-way southbound.

3. The motel parking lot has only one exit, and that is onto Route 1. Since it is a divided highway, only right turns are allowed from the parking lot onto the road.

4. Due to a marching band contest today, Pine is closed from this point west, and Main is closed from this point south.

5. Because of all the local events, this section of 6th Avenue will be open to cross traffic today only.

6. This is the only entrance to the park. Everyone must enter here, then proceed to the indicated ball field (GOAL).

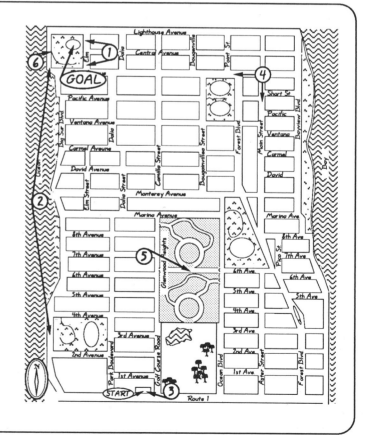

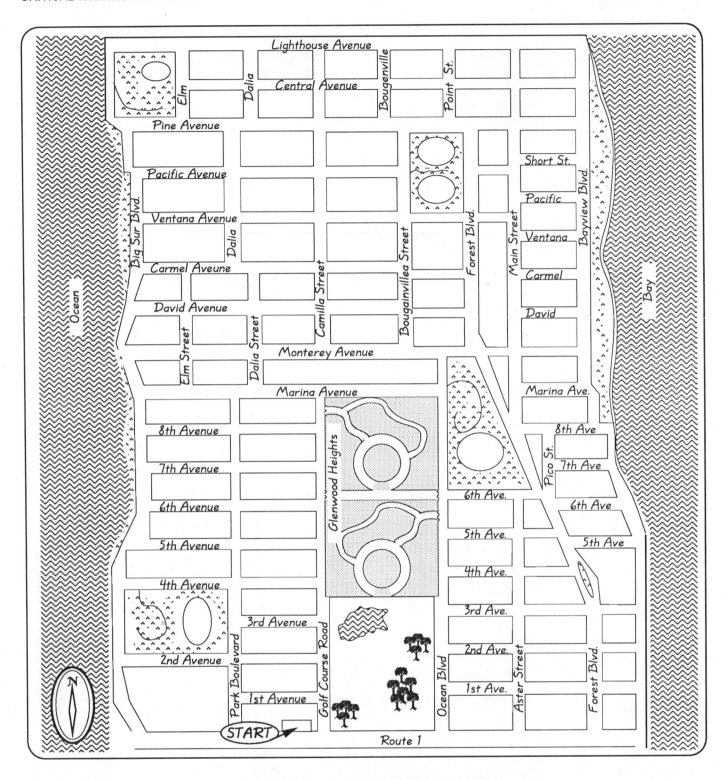

## BASEBALL CHAMPIONSHIP

Welcome to the State World Series! Your team has won its district championship and is in Atlantic Grove to compete for the state title. You and your friends are staying at the Butterfly Motel (START). You have a map (above), but only the coach knows at which ball park the team is to play today. He will give you written directions for getting from the motel to the park. These directions include important local information that is not on your printed map.

## THE BAKERY • 1
### Writer Information

Direct your reader from the starting point to the goal. You have the following knowledge that is not available on the reader's map. Mark your copy of the map, then create and describe a path to the goal.

1   Today's job will be cookie making. First get the ingredients from the cupboard and the refrigerator.

2   Next, the ingredients should be put into a mixer.

3   After mixing, the cookies should be put on baking pans.

4   The baking pans can then be put into an oven.

5   After they are baked, the cookies need to be decorated.

6   When you have put the cookies into the display cases in the store, you may leave for the day through the shop door.

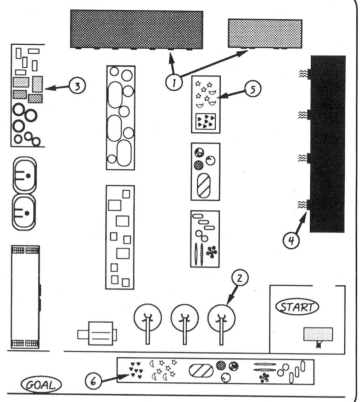

## THE BAKERY • 2
### Writer Information

Direct your reader from the starting point to the goal. You have the following knowledge that is not available on the reader's map. Mark your copy of the map, then create and describe a path to the goal.

1   Today's job will be bread packaging and cleanup. First take the bread out of the oven.

2   Next take the bread to the slicer.

3   Then the sliced bread must be put into packages.

4   Once it's packaged, the bread goes into the freezer.

5   After everything is done, all utensils must be washed.

6   Finally, pick up your paycheck for the day's work and leave through the shop door.

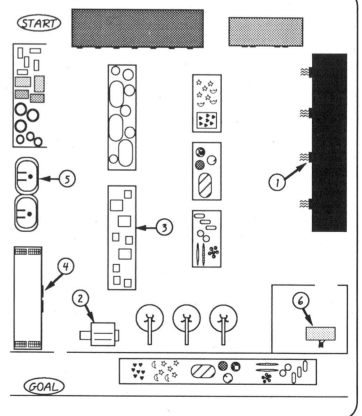

          © 1989 MIDWEST PUBLICATIONS • P.O. Box 448, Pacific Grove, CA  93950

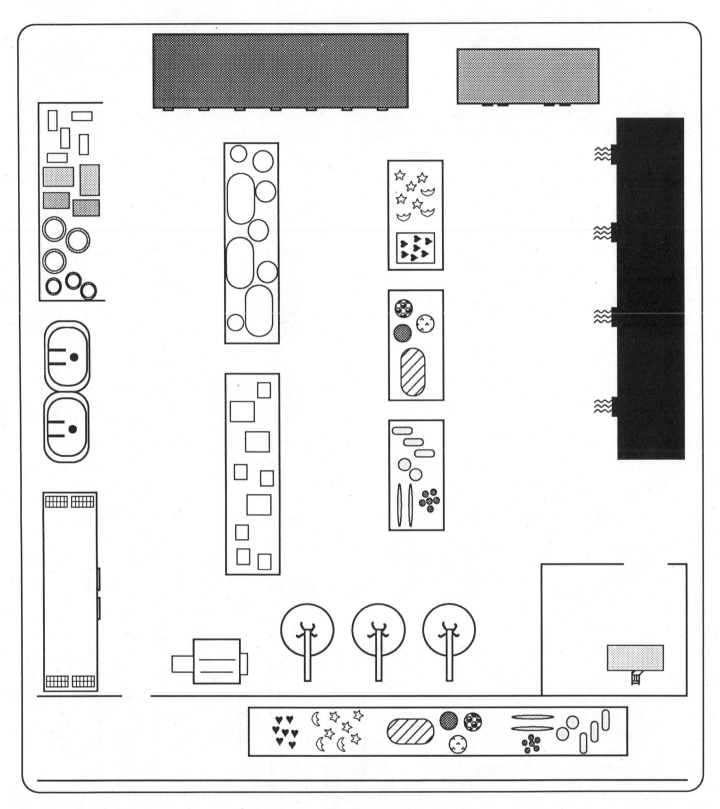

## THE BAKERY

Congratulations! You have just been given a new job at a bakery. There are many things you will need to do in order to finish your day's work. Your boss, the manager, will be giving you a list explaining how to do your job. Good luck.

## THE CITY LIBRARY • 1
### Writer Information

Direct your reader from the starting point to the goal. You have the following knowledge that is not available on the reader's map. Mark your copy of the map, then create and describe a path to the goal.

1   Tell Hornrim where to get a library card from the librarian.
2   Then tell Hornrim where to find the card catalog so the books needed can be found on the shelves.
3   Next tell Hornrim what sections to look in to find the books.
4   There is only one place left to sit. Tell Hornrim where it is located and that you will be saving it.
5   Tell Hornrim where to do some typing.
6   You need to tell Hornrim two final things: where to check out the books and how to get out of the library.

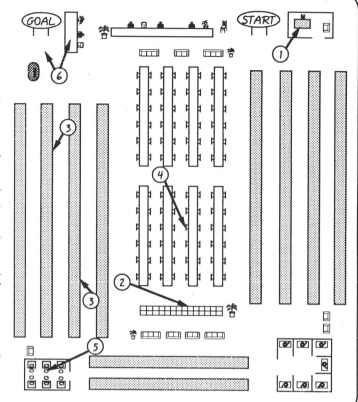

## THE CITY LIBRARY • 2
### Writer Information

Direct your reader from the starting point to the goal. You have the following knowledge that is not available on the reader's map. Mark your copy of the map, then create and describe a path to the goal.

1   Tell Hornrim where to find a record.
2   Next tell Hornrim where to go to listen to the record.
3   Help Hornrim find the right place to go to get a reference book.
4   Help Hornrim find a comfortable place to sit and read the reference book.
5   Tell Hornrim where to find the book return and the way out of the library.

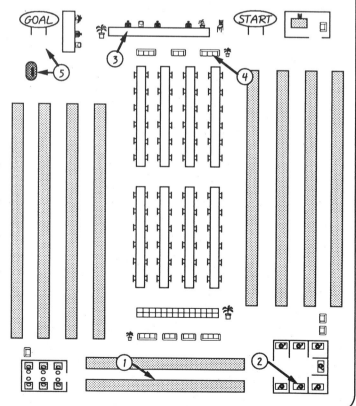

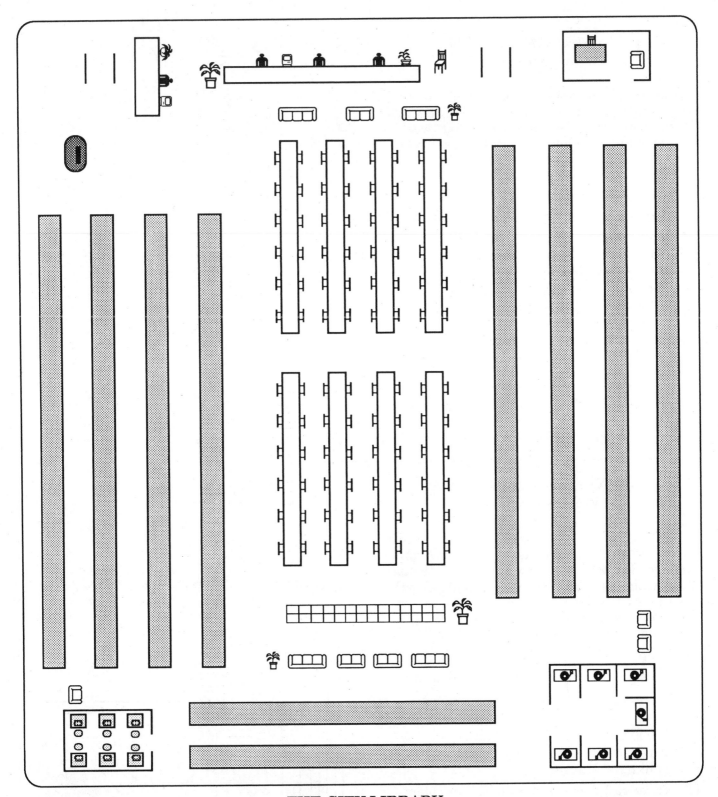

## THE CITY LIBRARY

Your family, the Hornrims, has moved to a new city and you want to use the city library. Since you have never been to this library before, your neighbor has offered to help you. You have given your neighbor a list of what you need. Your neighbor will now go to the library with you and tell you how to use the library services.

### NEW TOWN OF MIKIEVILLE • 1
### Writer Information

Your friend has sent you a map of his new community along with an invitation to visit. He has included information about last week's storm damage. You must walk along roads and footpaths to his house, as the storm has washed out or flooded many areas.

1   Get off at this train station.
2   Pedestrians may not use this overpass.
3   This overpass has collapsed. It is safe to walk across the corner of the marsh to get onto the road again.
4   This road is unsafe due to a big sinkhole.
5   This is your friend's house.

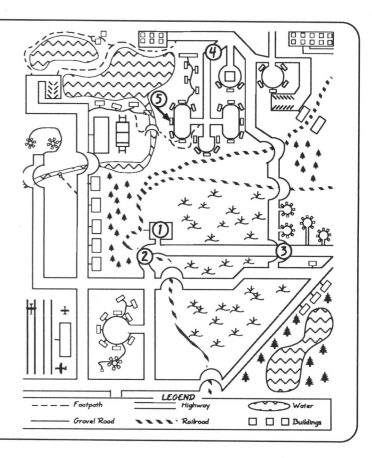

### NEW TOWN OF MIKIEVILLE • 2
### Writer Information

Your family has just moved to a community, and your sister is arriving on a train from her college. She does not know how to find the new house. She must walk along roads and footpaths, as the area is quite marshy. On your way to a ballgame, you will meet her to give her a map and some special instructions.

1   Your sister's train will arrive here.
2   This road is closed while an old bridge is being repaired.
3   Path barricaded. Rare frogs are crossing to the other lake.
4   An overturned truck has caused a chemical spill here. Unsafe area.
5   River-raft docks. Ride raft past problem.
6   No pedestrians allowed along the shoulders of this road.
7   New house.

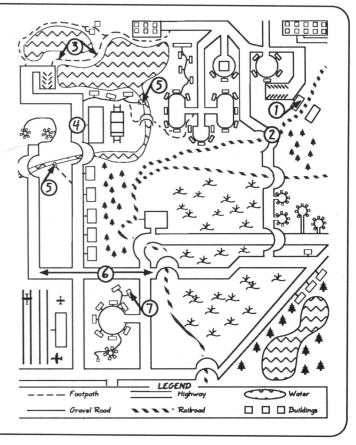

© 1989 MIDWEST PUBLICATIONS • P.O. Box 448, Pacific Grove, CA  93950

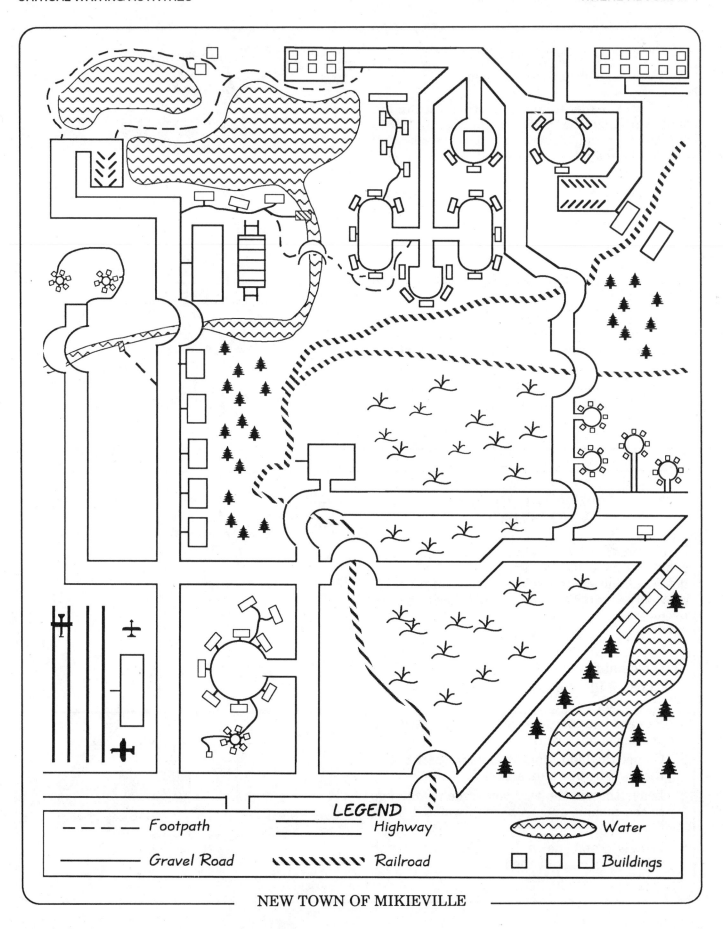

## LEGEND

- - - - - Footpath
———— Gravel Road
———— Highway
〰〰〰 Railroad
⬭ Water
▢ ▢ ▢ Buildings

NEW TOWN OF MIKIEVILLE

## SPACE SHUTTLE • 1
### Writer Information

Direct your reader from the starting point to the goal. You have the following knowledge that is not available on the reader's map. Mark your copy of the map, then create and describe a path to the goal.

1   To continue the tour, first go to the electrical storage area to look at the shuttle's huge generators and batteries.

2   Next, find the entrance to the shuttle's laboratory.

3   Then go to the cages and observe the laboratory animals.

4   Next, leave the shuttle lab and make your way to the cockpit.

5   Sit in this seat and learn how some of the instruments work.

6   Finally, come down from the cockpit and rejoin your class at the tour office.

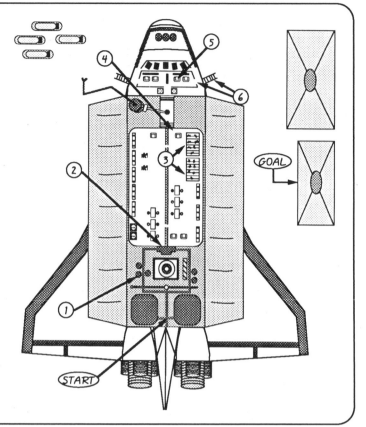

## SPACE SHUTTLE • 2
### Writer Information

Direct your reader from the starting point to the goal. You have the following knowledge that is not available on the reader's map. Mark your copy of the map, then create and describe a path to the goal.

1   To continue the tour, go down into the cargo bay, look around, and come back through the same hatch

2   Next, find the entrance to the shuttle laboratory.

3   Proceed to a computer bank and watch it run programs for a while.

4   Go pet the laboratory rabbits in their cages, then wash your hands at sink.

5   Leave the lab the way you came in, then go to the cockpit and sit here to watch a short film.

6   Finally, come down from the cockpit and rejoin your class at the bus.

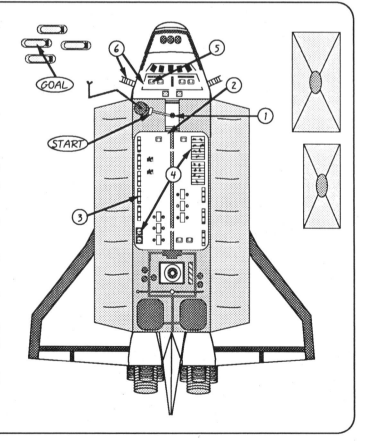

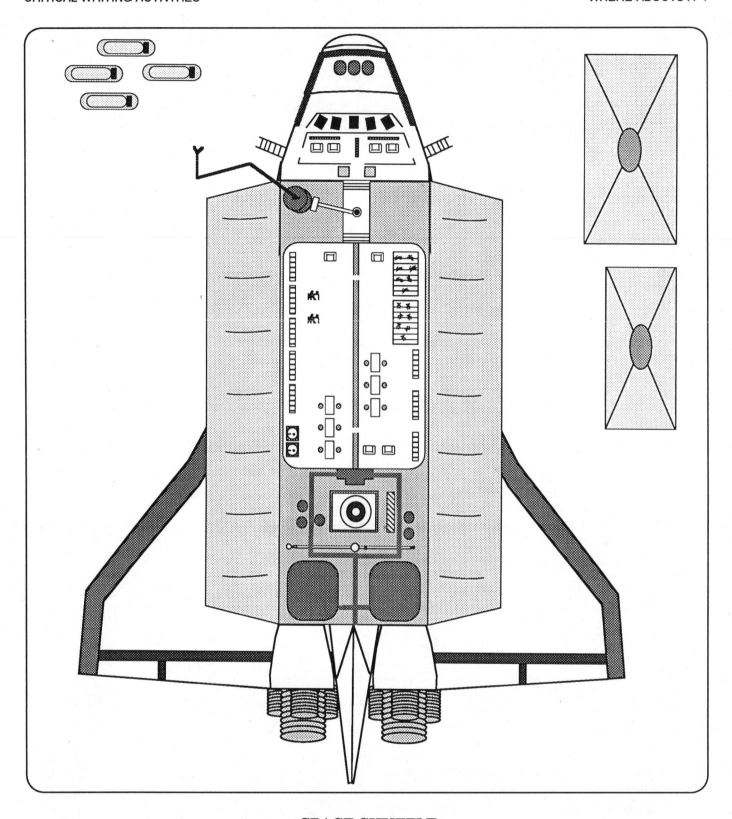

## SPACE SHUTTLE

You are a student from a science class touring a space shuttle. Somehow you get lost and find yourself separated from your group and in the wrong part of the ship. Fortunately, you meet a crewperson who writes you directions about how to finish the tour and get back to your group.

## DESERT MOTOCROSS RACE • 1
### Writer Information

Direct your reader from the starting point to the goal. You have the following knowledge that is not available on the reader's map. Mark your copy of the map, then create and describe a path to the goal.

1   First checkpoint – fill canteens with fresh water.

2   Rule – cross the river under the water without getting wet.

3   Second checkpoint – fill the motorcycle with gas.

4   Trick – get over the mountains to the next checkpoint without taking any roads.

5   Third checkpoint – sign a deal with a movie producer who is waiting for you at a cafe on the end of a pier.

6   Rule – get the right equipment, then go through the lava gorge to the goal.

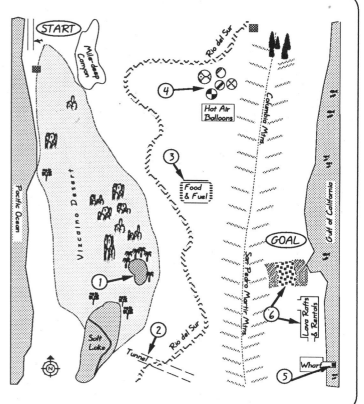

## DESERT MOTOCROSS RACE • 2
### Writer Information

Direct your reader from the starting point to the goal. You have the following knowledge that is not available on the reader's map. Mark your copy of the map, then create and describe a path to the goal.

1   First checkpoint – pick up a raft and start traveling downriver.

2   Trick – water becomes too dangerous here because of rapids. Get off the river.

3   Trick – the desert is surrounded by high cliffs. The only way to get in is by a bridge over the Salt Lake.

4   Rule – pick some exotic cactus fruit to prove you were here.

5   Final checkpoint – drop off the motorcycle, then take a bus to the airport.

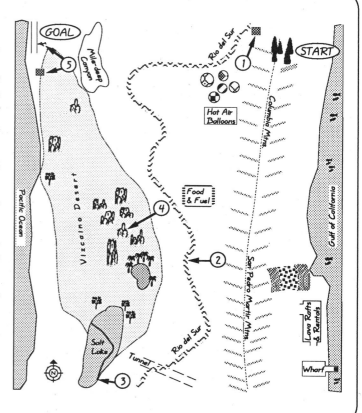

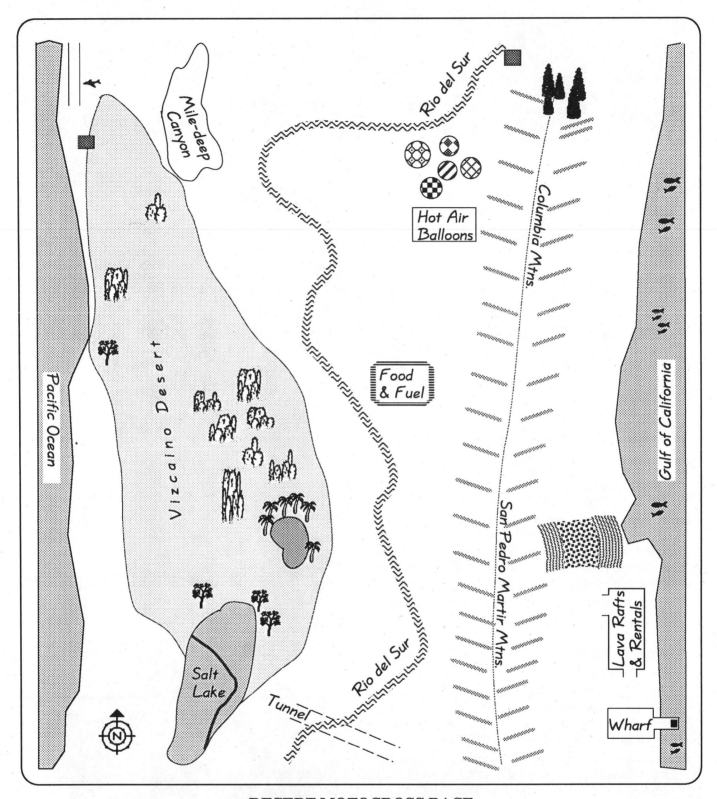

## DESERT MOTOCROSS RACE

You and a friend are contestants in a desert motocross race. You are the driver and your friend is the navigator. As you go through the course, there are checkpoints you must go through, rules to follow, and tricks for winning the race which only the navigator knows. These tasks must be fulfilled if you are to win.

## ELORAC'S NEBULA • 1
### Writer Information

Direct your reader from start to goal and back to the starting point. You have the following knowledge that is not available on the reader's map. Mark your copy of the map, then create and describe a path to the goal.

1  Area subject to asteroid showers which will puncture a space suit.

2  This entire area is a thick radioactive particle cloud—impossible to get through without a Two-ton Independent Personnel Transporter (TIPT).

3  Aliens have been sighted here. They are not, repeat, not, friendly!

4  A newly discovered Black Hole. Get too close and you'll get sucked into it!

5  Spare ion particles found here are useful for fuel in an TIPT.

6  Abandoned TIPT here is still usable, but you'll have to get fuel to go anywhere.

7  Colony location. Get spare parts here.

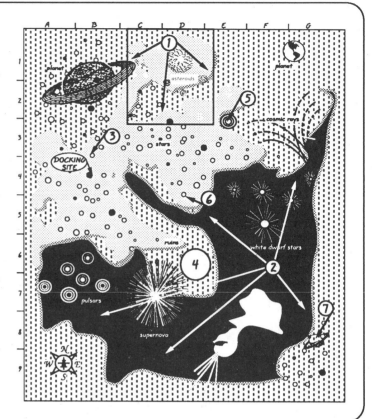

## ELORAC'S NEBULA • 2
### Writer Information

Direct your reader from start to goal and back to the starting point. You have the following knowledge that is not available on the reader's map. Mark your copy of the map, then create and describe a path to the goal.

1  This mystery gas cloud has not yet been explored, but initial tests indicate that it might be poisonous to human beings.

2  Area contaminated by radiation; unsafe.

3  Solar flares near here make this area too hot for unprotected humans.

4  These ruins are from early alien culture, not built by explorers from your solar system. Extremely unsafe buildings.

5  Humans can only go three grid sections in any direction on a single tank of oxygen. and can carry no more than two tanks at a time. Drop empty tanks as you go, but use up all of each tank.

6  Spare oxygen tank locations.

7  Colony location. Get spare parts here.

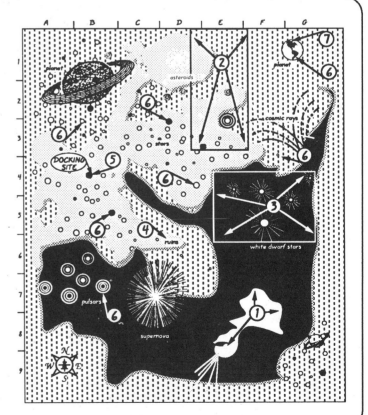

© 1989 MIDWEST PUBLICATIONS • P.O. Box 448, Pacific Grove, CA 93950

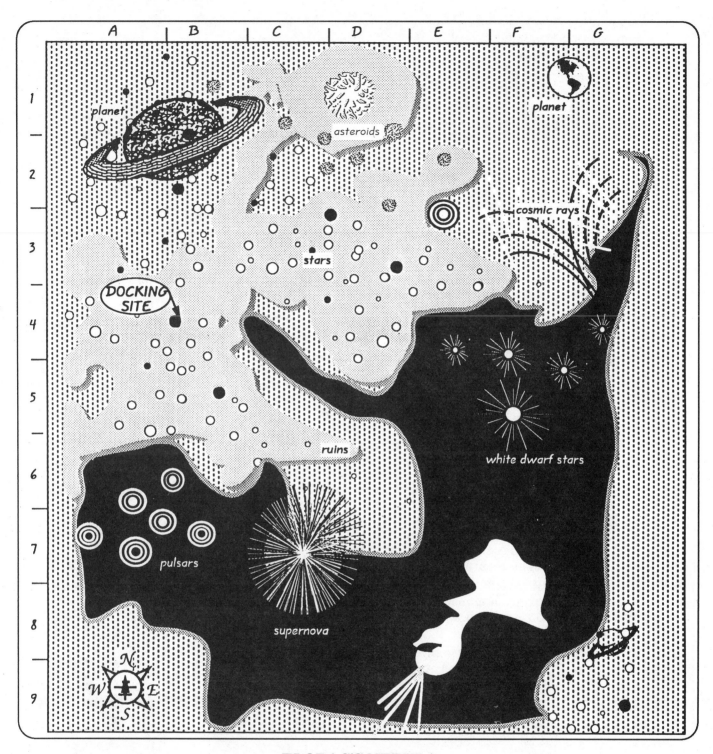

## ELORAC'S NEBULA

You have just docked your crippled space yacht at the Unified Nations site in Elorac's Nebula. You are not the first, however, for you can see the remains of an older ship from your viewing room. According to your computer, earlier explorers established a colony, then were never heard from again. You have a map of the area (above), a space suit, and a full tank of oxygen, but can find no colony on the map. When you explore the old ship, you find some written directions, but no marked map. You need to find the colony, get parts for your yacht, then return to the landing site so you can repair the yacht, and finish your trip.

## SUMMER VACATION • 1
### Writer Information

Direct your reader from the starting point to the goal. You have the following knowledge that is not available on the reader's map. Mark your copy of the map, then create and describe a path to the goal.

1   Living History Farms demonstrate farm life of the late 1800s and that of the future.

2   The Amana Colonies, seven villages with interesting museums and good restaurants. Craftsmen here make yarn, weave fabrics, and build furniture.

3   The Herbert Hoover National Historic Site and Presidential Library.

4   Hannibal—home of Mark Twain and setting for many of his famous novels.

5   Lake of the Ozarks Recreation Area— swimming, boating, and water skiing.

6   Road closed at this point due to construction and resurfacing.

7   Optional side trip to visit the zoo, the Arch, and the Botanical Gardens, and see a baseball game at Busch Stadium.

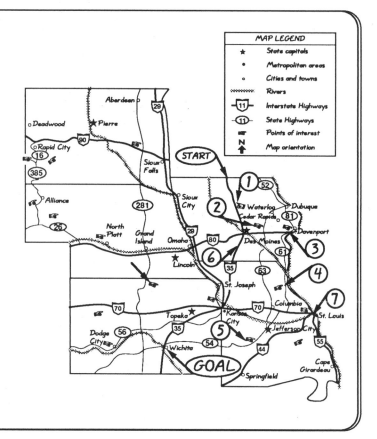

## SUMMER VACATION • 2
### Writer Information

Direct your reader from the starting point to the goal. You have the following knowledge that is not available on the reader's map. Mark your copy of the map, then create and describe a path to the goal.

1   Living History Farms demonstrate farm life of the late 1800s, as well as a farm of the future.

2   Chimney Rock National Historic Site.

3   Scout's Rest Ranch, home of William "Buffalo Bill" Cody, is here.

4   The Agate Fossil Beds here are fascinating.

5   Spring floods washed out several bridges north of this point on the interstate.

6   Beautiful country, including Black Hills National Forest and Mt. Rushmore. A giant sculpture, the Crazy Horse Memorial, is being carved out of a mountain here.

7   Badlands National Monument is a favorite tourist attraction, but there aren't many places to buy gasoline or food. Be sure to stop in town before you go there.

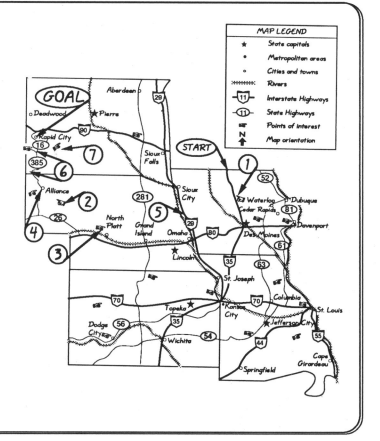

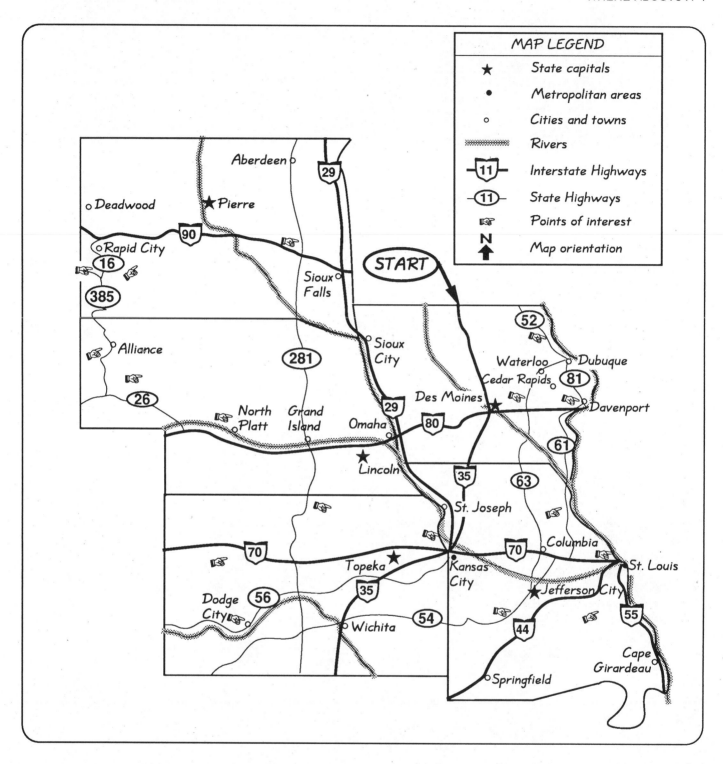

## SUMMER VACATION

It's June, and you and your family are planning a summer vacation trip. For five years, you have written to a pen pal in another state, and your parents have said that you will be going close to your pen pal's house on your trip. You have written to your friend to ask for suggestions of routes, things to see, and places to avoid on your trip. The map above is the only one available to you, and it has some key information missing. All points of interest do have access roads, but they are not shown on the map.